DISABLED PEOPLE

This edition produced in 1995

Designed and produced by
Aladdin Books Ltd, 28 Percy Street, London W1P 0LD

Design: Rob Hillier
Editor: Jen Green
Picture research: Emma Krikler
Consultant: Angela Grunsell

Pete Sanders is senior lecturer in health education at the University of North London. He was a head teacher for ten years and has written many books on social issues for children.

Angela Grunsell is an advisory teacher specialising in development education and resources for the primary school age range.

The publishers would like to acknowledge that the photographs reproduced in this book have been posed by models or have been obtained from photographic agencies.

A CIP record for this book is available from the British Library.

First published in Great Britain in 1991 by
Watts Books, 96 Leonard Street, London EC2A 4RH

ISBN: 0 7496 0635 5 (hardback)
ISBN: 0 7496 2071 4 (paperback)

Printed in Belgium

"LET'S TALK ABOUT"

PETE SANDERS

Gloucester Press
London · New York · Sydney

We all have different abilities. But schools and all kinds of places are not always adapted to suit the needs of people, including those with disabilities, who want to attend.

"Why talk about disabled people?"

If you look at your friends and the people you know at school or at home, you will realise that all of us have different abilities. You may have a friend who is good at maths, whilst you find it difficult. Or perhaps you enjoy running, but have a friend who cannot run very fast. Have you ever been picked out at school because you were unable to do something? If so, you will be able to understand what it feels like to be judged by what you can't do instead of what you can.

One in every ten people in the world has a disability. Often people with disabilities are seen as merely disabled, instead of as individuals. This can sometimes mean that they are ignored, or treated with less respect than others. Disabled people do not always have the same opportunities as people without a disability. We all have special needs. This book will help you develop some understanding of what it might mean to have a disability.

Many people think it is a good idea for children of different abilities to go to the same school. They feel that this will help us all to understand one another better.

“What do we mean by disability?”

You will know that the brain is sometimes described as the control centre of the body. It is the brain which sends the signals which make your body work. If someone is physically disabled, this usually means that a part of the body is not able to respond to the signals sent by the brain. This is because that part of the body has been damaged in some way. If you have ever broken your ankle, you will know how this feels.

There are many kinds of physical disability. Some you may already know about, such as blindness or deafness. Others you may not have heard of, for instance, paraplegia, which is caused by damage to the spine.

If the brain is not able to send clear messages to parts of the body, or is itself damaged, this may mean that a person is mentally disabled. This can make him or her less able to think clearly, or to express ideas and feelings in the same way as others. It may mean he or she learns at a slower rate.

Some people are disabled from the time they are born. They may have inherited a condition from their parents, such as muscular dystrophy, which causes wasting of the muscles. Others may have had an accident, or an illness such as polio, which caused their disability. Some disabilities can be cured, others cannot. With some illnesses, the disability may become worse as time goes on. This is often the case with multiple sclerosis, a disease which can attack the central nervous system.

It is easy to confuse disability with inability. Just because someone is disabled does not necessarily mean that he or she cannot do certain things. Able-bodied people sometimes assume things about disabled people. For instance, they may think that a person who cannot talk because of a physical disability is also mentally disabled. Some disabled people often communicate in ways which may seem strange to you. You know that doing something in a different way is not the same as being unable to do it at all.

You can't always tell by looking at someone whether they are disabled or not. Some disabilities, such as deafness, are called "hidden" disabilities for this reason.

“If people have a disability, what difficulties do they have to overcome?”

You already know that one of the biggest difficulties disabled people face is the attitude of other people. Often because of their own feelings of fear or ignorance, some people treat those with a disability as if they are not there. Others may try to do too much. Their intentions may be good, but their actions can sometimes be upsetting to the disabled person. You know the feeling you get if an adult talks down to you, assumes that you can’t do something or treats you as if you were much younger than you really are. This kind of prejudice has often meant that disabled people have found it difficult to find work, even though there is a law in this country which says that larger companies have to employ a certain number of people with a disability.

Apart from other people’s attitudes, a disabled person may have mixed feelings about their disability. Being disabled may involve making a lot of changes, and this takes time.

A physically disabled boy works with a physiotherapist to strengthen his muscles and improve movement. The day-to-day life of a disabled person may demand an enormous effort.

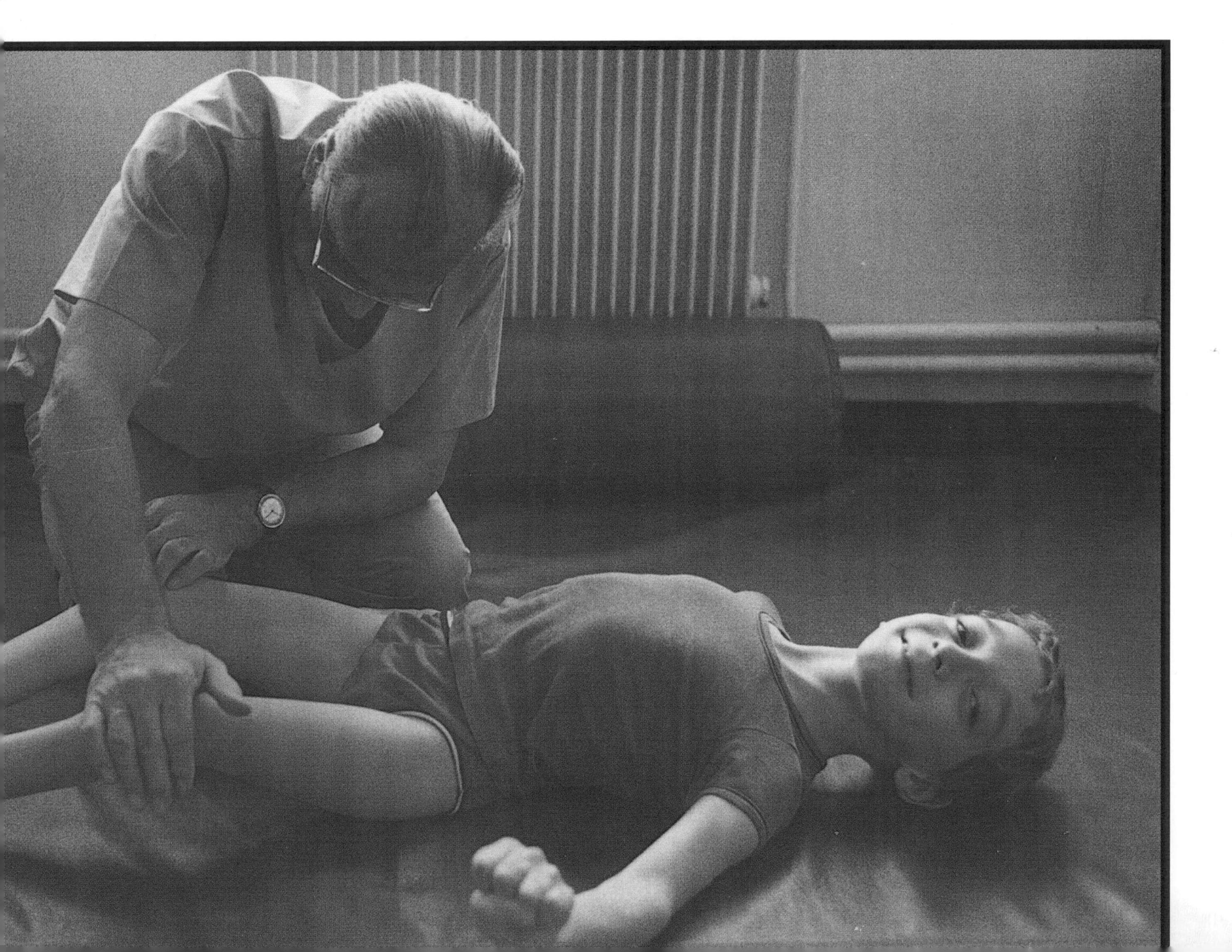

Life is not always arranged with the needs of disabled people in mind. Making the necessary adjustments takes both time and money. You have probably seen people in wheelchairs, or wearing hearing aids. Everyday objects, and workplaces of all kinds, can be adapted so that they can be used by disabled people. Lower kitchen units for use by people in wheelchairs, and books in Braille, a system of representing words as raised dots on the page, are two examples. But often disabled people do not have enough money to afford the special equipment, or the care, that they need.

If you think about the layout of your local cinema or sports centre, you might understand how difficult it is sometimes for physically disabled people to use such buildings. They often have steps in front of them, or narrow doorways, or lots of steps inside. If access is provided for physically disabled people, it is often not the same as for able-bodied people. Having to be carried upstairs, or sit at the side of the aisle in a cinema, can be quite embarrassing for some disabled people.

Many public places do not provide access for people with disabilities. Even when there is access, it may not be offered on the same terms as for people without disabilities.

“What help is available for people with a disability?”

Not all disabled people need any more help than the rest of us. For those who do, some help is available. Unfortunately, not everyone gets all the help they need. Sometimes this may be because disabled people are unwilling or even scared to ask for help. Often, though, it is not as easy to get help as it should be.

Some disabled people don’t always know what help they can get, or how to go about getting it. Some of the money which people pay to the government in taxes is used to help disabled people buy the special equipment they need. Others may receive help from charities. There are self-help groups and special classes for all kinds of disability. There are also organisations which encourage disabled and non-disabled people to join in a variety of activities together. Many believe that the best kind of help is that which does not make disabled people feel separate or isolated.

Some disabled people may have different ways of doing things. Maybe we should see people with disabilities as differently abled rather than as "disabled".

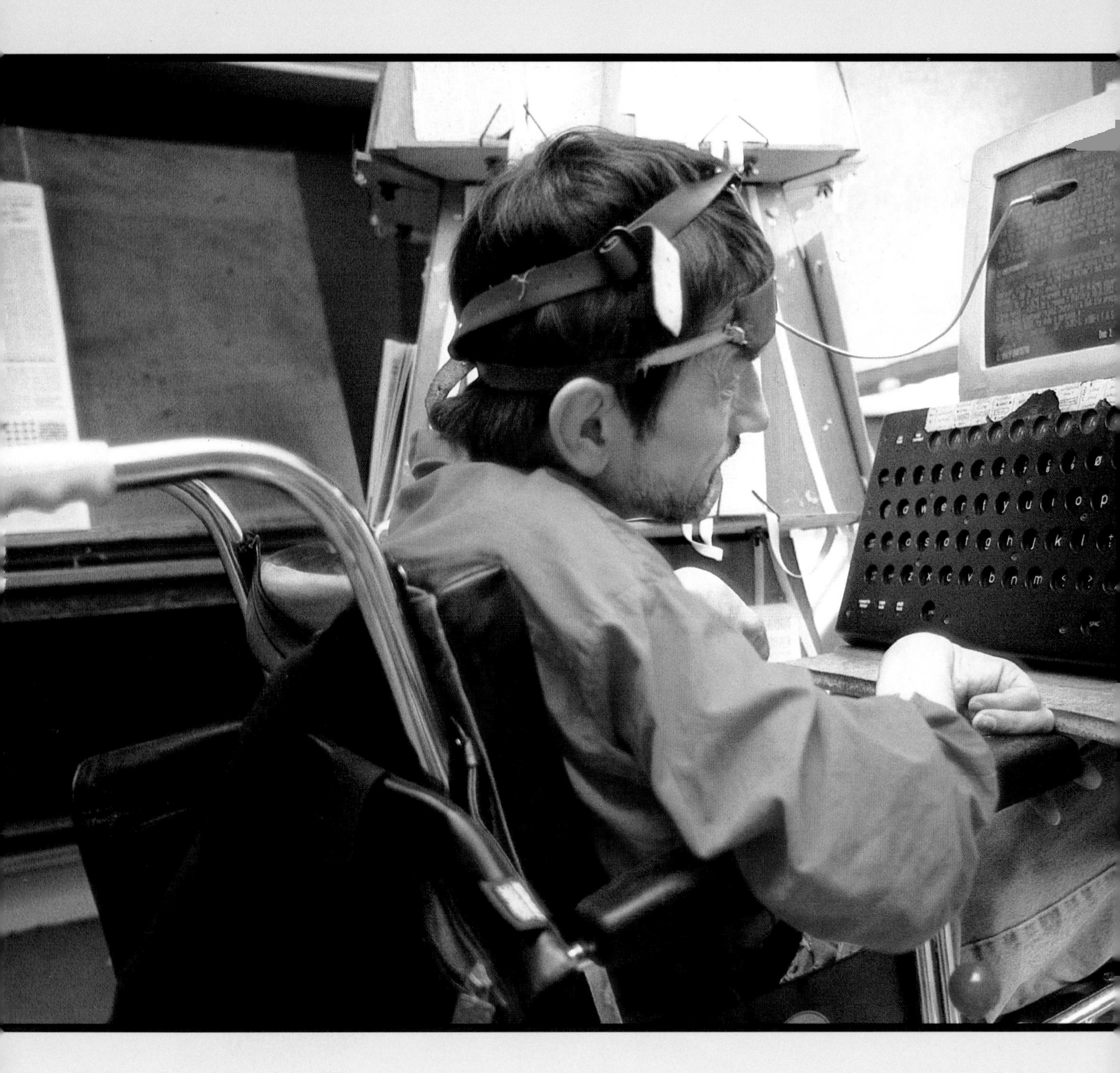

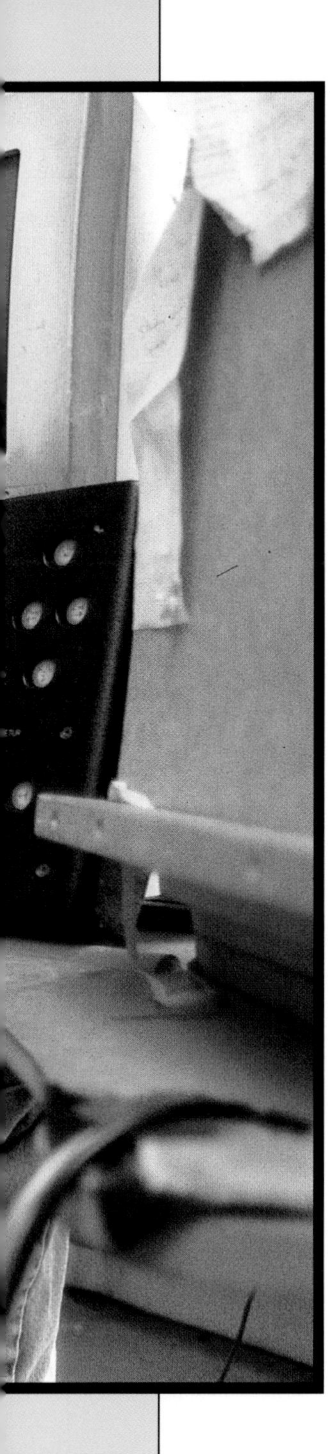

People who are severely disabled may need special treatment. They may need full-time attention from a carer. This is often a member of the person's family. If you have ever had to look after a brother or sister who was ill, you may be able to understand that caring for someone full-time can be stressful. Even people who enjoy being carers and get a lot out of caring for a disabled person may sometimes feel resentment at having to be there all the time. It can be just as difficult for the disabled person, who has to rely on another member of the family to do things for them.

Counselling services can help people to work through these feelings. There are also groups who organise holidays for disabled people, or who come in to look after a disabled person's needs for a short while, so that the carer can have time off. Unfortunately, this service is not available to everyone, and costs money to run. Many people believe that more of the money raised from taxes should be used to provide assistance to disabled people to get what they need.

A wordprocessor can be operated by a disabled person using a headpiece to strike the keys. All kinds of equipment can be adapted for use by people with disabilities.

“Should disabled people be treated in a special way?”

Has anyone ever tried to finish a task for you when you wanted to finish it yourself? If so, you will know how annoying it is when people start to join in without first asking you if you need any help. Disabled people are often treated in this way. Perhaps this is because people are not always sure how they should behave towards those with disabilities. Some people may feel embarrassed, or even frightened, particularly if a disabled person looks, or acts, very differently from the way they do. They may perhaps feel self-conscious, or even somehow guilty that the other person is disabled, and they are not.

We live in a society which often seems to want us to fit in with everyone else, and tends to be uncomfortable with things that are different. Disabled people are very rarely shown in advertisements on television. If they are, it is usually to make people feel sad for them.

Some sporting events welcome people of all abilities. By starting a short time before the runners on foot, wheelchair users are able to take part in marathons.

When we see disabled people, we sometimes think about how we might feel if we were disabled. This may help to explain why disabled people are sometimes pitied, instead of being treated as people with feelings.

Some disabled people may need to be treated in a special way. It depends what their disability is. You only have to think about how you would talk with someone if they came from a different country and spoke little of your language. This would mean that you would need to speak clearly, and perhaps more slowly. You might even use sign language.

It is important to find out what would be most helpful to the other person, instead of assuming that you know. This may take time. Some people become impatient. Others may be too selfish to make the effort. Remember that disabled people may do things in a slightly different way to you. All it needs is a little thought.

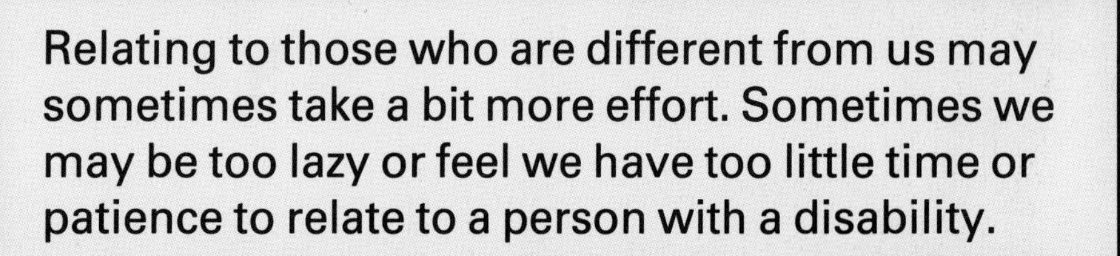

Relating to those who are different from us may sometimes take a bit more effort. Sometimes we may be too lazy or feel we have too little time or patience to relate to a person with a disability.

"How should I treat someone with a disability?"

We are all different and special in our own way. Have you ever been annoyed when someone has called you by your brother or sister's name by mistake, or said that you looked just like another member of the family? People sometimes forget that we are all unique. We are all good at different things. Perhaps we should define people as differently abled rather than as disabled or able-bodied.

You may like to help others. It is important to know when and when not to offer help. If you are not used to being with disabled people, you may feel embarrassed or uncomfortable at first. Talking about your feelings can help.

You have probably heard people calling each other names. Because of their prejudice or ignorance, the words they use are sometimes the ones that describe people with different disabilities. You know that this is hurtful, unkind and unfair. It is similar to calling people names that are racist.

Electric wheelchairs enable some disabled people to get about. Many disabled people need no help at all to get on with their daily lives. Others would welcome your offer of help.

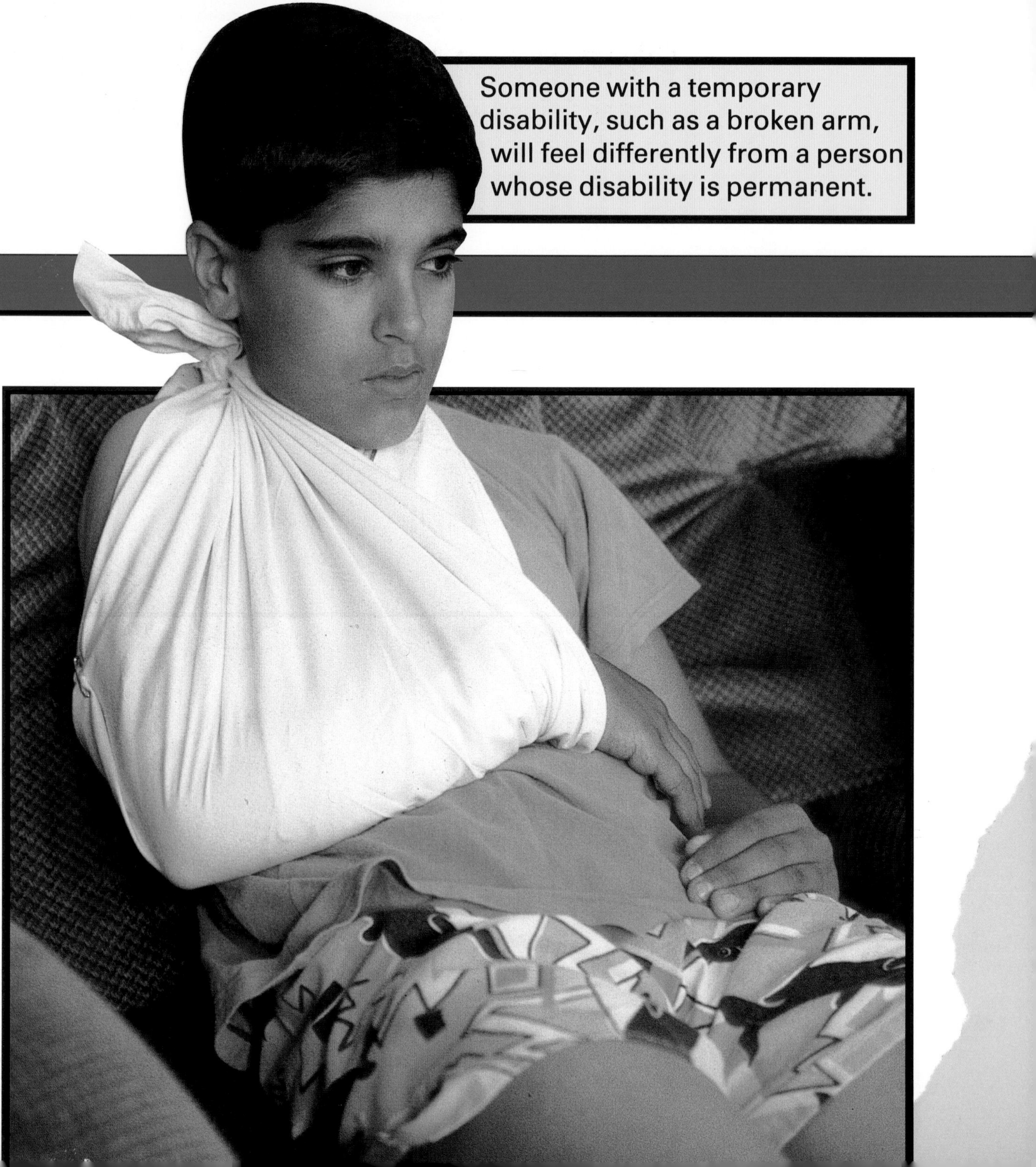

Someone with a temporary disability, such as a broken arm, will feel differently from a person whose disability is permanent.

"How do people feel about being disabled?"

We all feel different things at different times. You will remember how sometimes you may be quite confident about trying something new. At other times you might feel nervous, and find a task which is familiar very hard to do. The way disabled people feel about their disability will depend on the circumstances of the individual. Of course, it also depends if the money is available that will allow them to live their life the way they want to.

People who have been disabled for a long time may have adapted well to their situation. But there may still be things which they find difficult to accept and adjust to. People who have become disabled recently, perhaps after an accident, may need time to come to terms with their new life. Sometimes disabled people may feel depressed. They may even occasionally feel angry at the people closest to them, such as their families or friends.

Have you ever hurt your arm, and found it frustrating not to be able to do things which you usually find easy? For some people who have been recently disabled, it is a case of having to learn to do things again, perhaps in a different way. It can be very difficult for somebody who has to have special help, and yet does not want to be treated differently from anyone else. Some people disguise the fact that they have a disability, because of the way society often treats disabled people.

Many people with disabilities have come to terms with being disabled. Some have learned to treat their disability as a matter of fact. They get on with their lives. They are determined that their disability is not going to get in the way of enjoying life to the full. Some say that their disability has helped them become stronger and has given them a sense of determination. Others feel that having a disability has given them skills and insights they would not otherwise have had. Some join organisations which are trying to give disabled people exactly the same opportunities as others.

Many people with disabilities adjust by learning new skills. The picture shows a boy with a hearing disability who is communicating with the aid of both sign language and a hearing device.

“What can we learn from disabled people?”

We can all learn from each other, whether disabled or not. Disabled people don’t necessarily see themselves as courageous. They probably feel that they have simply adapted to their situation. This may have taken a lot of effort. They have learned not to give up, but to keep on trying. Perseverance and being able to adapt are important to us all.

Life isn’t always fair. At some time, we all have to cope with difficult situations. Having to face up to a challenge can often help us to have a better understanding of ourselves and of other people.

Often people’s idea of disabled people is that they are very brave. If you know a disabled person, you may have been surprised at how ordinary their disability seems to them.

What can I do?

You now have a better understanding of how important it is to treat all people as individuals. It is not helpful to view disabled people as if they all have the same feelings and needs. Rather than rushing in to help, you know that it is better to find out first what kind of help the disabled person would welcome.

Disabled people are often shown as people to be pitied. You know that this can be offensive. Remember that words can hurt. Although name-calling can seem harmless to some people, you know that it is actually very unkind. It stops people from seeing the person instead of the disability. We all have different abilities. It is important to be aware of our own needs and sensitive to those of others.

Addresses for further information

RADAR (Royal Association of Disability and Rehabilitation)
25 Mortimer Street
London W1N 8AB
071 637 5400

DIAL UK (Disability Information & Advice Line)
Park Lodge, St Catherine's Hospital
Tick Hill Rd, Balby
Doncaster DN4 8QN
0302 310123

What the words mean

able-bodied describes a person who does not have a disability.

access is about whether it is possible for a disabled person in a wheelchair or on crutches to enter and move around in a building without help.

Braille is a system of reading through touch.

learning difficulty is when a person with a mental disability tends to take longer to learn something than someone who is not mentally disabled.

multiple sclerosis is a disease of the central nervous system.

muscular dystrophy is an inherited disease which causes weakening and wasting of the muscles.

paraplegia is a paralysis, or loss of movement, in the lower part of the body, caused by damage to the spine.

polio is a disease which attacks the spinal cord.

prejudice is having an opinion about someone or something without finding out about it for yourself – pre-judging an issue.

Index

Photographic Credits:
Cover and pages 8-9 and 14-15: Topham Picture Source; page 6-7: Science Photo Library; page 10-11: Frank Spooner Pictures; pages 4-5, 12, 16-17, 20-21 and 24: Marie-Helene Bradley; page 18-19: Paul Nightingale; pages 23 and 28: Spectrum Colour Library; page 26: Eye Ubiquitous.